AF885471

REFLECTIONS FROM DECADES OF PRACTICE IN PERSONAL INJURY LAW

INFORMATION THAT MAY HELP YOU ACHIEVE THE COMPENSATION YOU DESERVE AND PROVIDE YOU WITH INSIGHT INTO THE PROCESS

Robert I. Feinberg, Esq.

Copyright © 2016 by Robert I. Feinberg, Esq.

All rights reserved. No part of this book may be used or reproduced in any manner whatsoever without written permission of the author.

ISBN: 978-1-941645-82-6

Designed and Published by:

Speakeasy Publications
73-03 Bell Blvd, #10
Oakland Gardens, NY 11364
www.SpeakeasyMarketingInc.com
(888) 225-8594

Disclaimer

This publication is intended to be informational only. No legal advice is being given, and no attorney-client relationship is intended to be created by reading this material. If you are facing legal issues, whether criminal or civil, seek professional legal counsel to get your questions answered.

To my existing and future clients, to whom I wish the best recovery possible and to whom I pledge to work toward that end.

To my past clients, for whom I hope I represented in a way that generated confidence in the process and in me.

www.FeinbergAlban.com

Feinberg & Alban, P.C.
225 Franklin Street, 26th Floor
Boston, MA 02110

1051 Beacon Street
Brookline, MA, 02446
(617) 232-5950

A Small Sampling of Fabulous Reviews

Some of the Testimonials that Can Be Found Online:

"I highly recommend the Feinberg and Alban personal injury firm...wonderful people and representation. Attorney Robert Feinberg along with Attorney Alexis Cahill of Feinberg and Alban handled my personal injury case in which I was seriously injured through no fault of my own. They were compassionate, caring, hardworking, and dedicated the entire way through and are overall wonderful people. Also, the moral support I received from them was outstanding and unparalleled...especially during the early phases of my acute injuries which required subsequent major surgeries and the extensive rehabilitation and recovery periods that followed up until the very end. I can't thank them enough. I highly recommend Feinberg and Alban."

Tom

"Our case is closed and I'm going to miss him! Robert is a great person as well as an amazing lawyer. He responded to my inquiry through his website immediately. He came out to our home to make our meetings easier for our family. He took all the time we needed, to answer all of our questions. He always returned phone calls, texts, e-mails (whatever worked for us). He was always happy to talk to one, or all of us (he represented our young, adult son). He ALWAYS kept us informed and prepared for any upcoming events or expectations. I just can't find the one word to sum up our experience but I would choose him all over again."

Sue

"Robert is a great lawyer! I am so happy to have found Feinberg and Alban, and Robert as my lawyer. He cares very much for his clients and works very hard for them. He handled my case when I thought all was lost. I am so grateful to him. I will tell anyone that needs a good lawyer to call Feinberg and Alban and ask for Robert Feinberg. Thank you Robert."

Gwendolyn

Table Of Contents

AUTHOR INTRODUCTION

Robert I. Feinberg is a very well-known personal injury attorney in Massachusetts. He has practiced personal injury law exclusively in his 35 years as a lawyer. Robert has won numerous awards and recognitions, including the designation of Super Lawyer in the category of personal injury for all years that the honor has been given. Robert Feinberg is also a member of the Million Dollar Advocates Forum, Multi-Million Dollar Advocates Forum, and is included in the National Trial Lawyers Association Top 100 Trial Lawyers for Massachusetts.

Robert's verdict of almost 8 million dollars in a boiler explosion case was the highest verdict for a personal injury in Massachusetts over a five year period. The offer had been only $200,000. This superb result is not lost on insurance companies and causes them to offer Robert's clients more money than otherwise would be the case.

Robert has testified before the Massachusetts Joint House/Senate Insurance Committee on insurance coverage on several occasions. He has also lectured more than ten times to other attorneys on the handling of personal injury cases, especially concerning trial practice. His court pleadings have been used as a teaching tool for members of the American Association of Justice. Attorney Feinberg is a 25-year member of the Board of Governors of the Massachusetts Academy of Trial Attorneys. He is also a member of the Florida Bar. He has authored more than 300 blogs on the handling of personal injury cases, 75 of which are also presented in video format on the firm's website, www.feinbergalban.com.

Mr. Feinberg and the firm have an AV Preeminent rating from Martindale-Hubbell, the oldest peer rating service for lawyers. AV is the highest rating given to attorneys and law firms and Robert has had that rating for 20 years, a very significant accomplishment. He also has a perfect rating of "10" from AVVO.

Practice Areas

- Civil Litigation
- Personal Injury
- Premises Liability
- Products Liability
- Wrongful Death
- Injuries to Children
- Brain Injuries and Burn Injuries

Honors

- AV® Martindale-Hubbell® Peer Review Ratings™
- AVVO, perfect "10" rating
- Super Lawyer in all years of the existence of the award. Category: plaintiff's personal injury

Education

- Brown University, B.A., magna cum laude, with honors, 1978
- University of Pennsylvania, J.D., Excellence in Evidence

Member

- Board of Governor of Massachusetts Academy of Trial Attorneys, 1991-present
- American Bar Association
- American Association of Justice
- Also Admitted To Practice In Florida

Languages

- Russian

What Considerations Do I Have Before Filing A Lawsuit In Massachusetts?

Although there are several considerations that one must take into account before hiring an attorney to pursue a personal injury case on his/her behalf, an absolute necessity is to make sure that a lawsuit is brought prior to the expiration of the statute of limitations. This probably does not surprise you as lay people are very familiar with the concept of a statute of limitations. What may surprise would-be clients is that the preparation for a lawsuit may require the expenditure of time and money. Therefore, a consultation significantly before the statute of limitations expires is well-advised. Frankly, it is not enough to understand the conclusive and preclusive effect that the statute of limitations has. The point to remember is that a phone call to an attorney a few days before the expiration may not be enough to rescue your case.

In Massachusetts, the statute of limitations for filing a basic negligence action is three years, meaning that if a formal complaint is not filed with the court within three years from the time that your accident occurred, your case will be dismissed. However, three years is merely a guideline, as there are often cases involving a municipality, the

Massachusetts Bay Transit Authority, medical malpractice or some other exception to the general time limit, where the statute of limitations for a particular claim (or a "notice" provision) is less than three years. Therefore, contact an attorney as soon as possible to be protected.

Another consideration that may be overlooked by clients is venue, or where a person can bring suit. In Massachusetts state court, the venue is in the county where the accident occurred, where the plaintiff lives or where the defendant lives. A corporation, though not a natural person, has a residence as well. The pros and cons of filing suit in certain counties as opposed to others should be explained to clients. Venue is a huge consideration as any savvy attorney will tell you.

Finally, because this book is about accidents and injuries, medical treatment is necessarily involved. Considerations of treatment should be undertaken by the client. The attorney should not direct medical treatment. Doing so could have an adverse effect on the case as the attorney could be portrayed as "choreographing" the medical situation. That may also raise questions of ethics. I advise my clients therefore to "let me play with the cards that I am dealt."

Things To Know About Personal Injury Law

There are a number of disciplines that impact on a personal injury case. The primary area - the substantive area of law with which we are dealing - is tort law. That's the right to recover civilly for a wrong, for negligence, or for an intentional act. Tort law is the basic framework for what my firm and I do. Related to that is evidence law. You should expect your lawyer to know which of the facts will make it into a courtroom as evidence, how they will be presented, or, if offered by the other side and potentially damaging, how they will be kept out of the courtroom. Then there is insurance, which is a very crucial aspect of this business. That's because you really do need a deep pocket for the ability to recover on a case.

In addition to being mindful of tort, evidence, and insurance law, the capable lawyer must be aware of a number of other related legal fields, including civil procedure, and various statutes. Massachusetts has a very strong Consumer Protection Act, referred to as 93A, and if it involves wrongful acts of the insurance company, it's piggybacked into what's called 176D. Basically, 176D imposes on insurance companies the duty to act in good faith even as against third parties. 93A simply but powerfully says that unfair acts or practices in business or commerce are declared unlawful. That governs a lot of relationships that exist. This law is a powerful tool in the plaintiff's lawyer's arsenal. The fact that it can be used in third-party contexts, where you are effectively suing an insurer with whom you have no contractual relationship, is a real asset. Not every state's consumer protection law is as wide-ranging.

Of course, one size doesn't fit all in a tort case. For example, with an accident involving children, a serious lawyer will need to know, and argue on behalf of the client, the fact that children are held to a different standard from that of an adult. The law is more indulgent where children are concerned. A child is held to the standard of children of similar experience, age and intelligence as opposed to the "reasonable man" standard, which is used for all adults. Therefore, for children, it seems that the law imposes a mixture of the objective and subjective while for adults it imposes a single, objective standard.

All of these things are a calculation that a thorough and careful attorney has to make in terms of assessing a case and presenting a case.

Components Of A Viable And Strong Personal Injury Case

Who you represent makes a big difference. How does the person appear, how do they come across, are they likable, and are they believable? Those are all factors that are very important. Secondly, of course, are the facts of the injury. How was it sustained? Is it a kind of case where the facts suggest a victory for a plaintiff or for the defendant? Leaving aside who the person is, is it a case that seems like a liability case? Can you understand how this person sustained the accident? Thirdly, does it involve a case of significant injury, such that the other side will take note and be more apt to pay?

If it's an insignificant injury, that suggests that it will be treated as a nuisance case. An insurance company sizes up the plaintiff and the plaintiff's attorney. They will want to learn, if they don't know already, if the attorney with whom they are about to face is one who is capable and doesn't take nuisance cases. Therefore, you want three factors at the minimum to establish the threshold requirement for liability: a likeable client; understandable facts as to how the injury was sustained (sometimes referred to as the mechanism of injury); and a significant attorney representing you. I should also note that a significant injury can play a part, a helpful part, in the willingness of the other side to accept liability. As a result, I have often said that a major injury case can "boot strap" questionable liability.

Role of Evidence and Witnesses in an Injury Case

Since I started law school almost 40 years ago, my father, a lawyer, gave me advice that has put me in good stead. He said, "If you want to do tort law and if you want to try cases, you had better learn evidence." I became a specialist in hearsay, which is a major part of evidence law. Evidence is extremely important because it will govern what is admissible at a trial and what isn't. As is often noted, the vast majority of these cases settle before a trial but they are always assessed as if they are going to trial. The amount of money you are offered for a settlement will be determined by what you persuade an insurance company or defense lawyer of what their risk is. Naturally, the higher the risk for them at trial, the higher the settlement you will achieve.

A Way Powerful Evidence Can Be Used In Injury Cases

I was recently consulted on a case in which a young driver (with a history of reckless behavior involving alcohol) was entrusted with keys to a car by a parent. To compound the facts, this underage man was going to a party on a Friday night where alcohol would almost certainly be served. In tort cases, the general rule is that previous accidents or behavior cannot be used as evidence in the trial of the particular accident. Therefore, a person's driving record most likely will not come into consideration in an auto accident. The rule of thumb is that the driver's behavior at the time in question is what matters rather than his/her overall driving record. There can, however, be an exception to this rule, and it occurred in the case I was consulted. This involves a doctrine, called "negligent entrustment." When pursuing that claim, the skillful lawyer can use evidence of prior acts, such as bad driving and drinking. Thus in a negligent entrustment claim, a parent (or another) can be independently liable in the event that he/she has given the keys to a young driver, who has been known to drink and will be heading to a party where alcohol will be prevalent.

Massachusetts courts have addressed this issue and have said that if prior accidents are admissible evidence, they cannot be used in determining fault or negligence in the accident on trial. The judge will instruct a jury on this, giving what is called a limiting instruction so that the jury will not misuse this evidence to determine who was at fault in the auto collision that is the subject of the lawsuit. Leone v. Doran, 363 Mass. 1 (1973). But you should know that this information will be used in another sense, that being to advance the negligent entrustment claim.

It is also important to understand the separate concept of respondeat superior. This means that an employer will be held liable for negligent driving committed by an employee. Nothing I have mentioned in this chapter detracts from that principle.

In summary, when an auto case is on trial, the past driving record of the at-fault party is usually not admissible evidence. The exception to this occurs in situations involving negligent entrustment. You should have a lawyer who is conversant with general principles of law and their exceptions.

Four Characteristics of Witness Testimony

When a lay person testifies to what he or she has observed about an accident involving the client, I am sure to consider the following: the witness' ability to perceive, tell the truth, remember, and narrate. These are the criteria that I was taught in evidence class almost forty years ago and they are relevant today. In fact, they probably have been relevant for hundreds of years in trial practice.

The four factors may seem interrelated. No doubt they are. Perception is the ability of a witness to see what they think they see. In this sense, perception isn't always reality. Many people will attempt to describe events though they lacked a sufficient vantage point from which to see the relevant facts. Secondly, when a witness testifies, that individual takes an oath, as we all know. Regrettably, some people have biases which influence their testimony, and others may not consciously set out to mislead but have been influenced by

extraneous factors. Third, the passage of time dims many a memory and, of course, depositions and trials take place many months, and usually many years, after the event causing the injury. Finally, the ability to describe what happened varies markedly with the skill of the witness. But by the way, after thirty-five years of practice, I have learned that this ability is not directly related to educational attainment.

In assessing prospective witness testimony, a lawyer could do far worse than keeping these four factors in mind.

Factors That Determine Value Of A Personal Injury Case

There are three important factors which determine the value of my clients' cases. The first two are expected but the third may surprise you.

Liability

The first is liability. How did the accident or injury happen? Who was at fault? And what was the conduct of both my client and the other party? These are essential questions in determining the extent of the liability or lack thereof.

Damages

The second issue is the damages. By this, we mean how badly was the client hurt and what the long-term effects are. Those effects include a broad range of things: loss of earning capacity, future medical costs, and pain and suffering, to name a few of the most obvious ones. Of course, the value of the case increases when there are greater damages, including specific damages (medical bills and loss of earning capacity) and general damages (pain and suffering). The people who provide the damages narrative will be the plaintiff himself/herself, lay witnesses with knowledge of the adverse effects of an injury on the client, and the medical expert(s).

Client's Personal Story

The third pillar is the client's personal story. This can only be ascertained by creating a close relationship with the client. This is done through personal meetings and getting a comprehensive understanding of their personal story. What is their background and biography? Not only do I find myself looking relatively far back in the past to the pre-injury days, but I also look at the manner in which a client responds to an accident or injury. The resulting limitations on their work and family life are important ways to understand how the client approaches life. It is essential for a lawyer to establish that his/her client is a hard working individual and, due to the negligence of the other party, is unable to work for the remainder of the client's life expectancy, assuming of course that that is so. But it is more involved than merely stating that the client is unable to work. A good lawyer will go further and convey how much pleasure and esteem the client derived from doing his/her job.

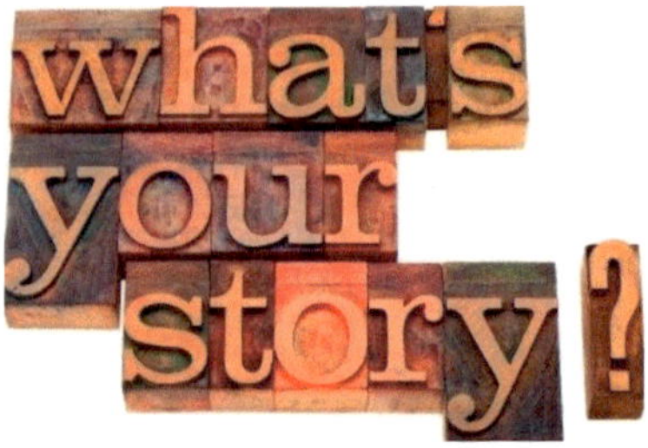

It is obviously essential to understand who you are representing. As indicated, frequent client contact is important. Again, bear in mind that there are also several sources a lawyer should use to understand the client's personal story. It is necessary to speak with family, friends, and co-workers. What is learned can go a long way toward achieving full compensation for the client.

Two injuries which occur in similar circumstances could have very different results. This can be explained, at least in part, on the lawyer's ability to understand, develop, and convey the client's story through seemingly little vignettes, among other things. Those clients in a personal injury action who do not get full compensation have likely not had their stories properly developed and told.

Importance Of Timely Medical Treatment In A Personal Injury Case

First of all, any person suffering a trauma should do what is medically necessary. It is never advisable for the person to over-treat. Quite simply, if the person is better or well, then they don't need more medical treatment. They shouldn't let the case be their guide. Conversely, if they are not well and if they have problems, they should get those medical problems checked out.

The guiding concern should be to advance their own medical recovery and not to focus on the implications for the case. In considering on whether to embark upon future medical treatment, a client should consider what an ethical lawyer says: "don't treat for purposes of the case." It's bad ethically and it's bad tactically. If an insurance person or a defense lawyer learns of it - that is, that the case is the reason for the treatment - it will be very harmful to the result.

The next point is about the proximity in time of medical treatment to the accident. It's common sense that the closer in time to the actionable event, the accident, that the injured party treats, the better it is for the case. There will then be documented injuries.

The above logic is particularly true in the case of a pre-existing condition. Insurers are poised to blame everything on that pre-existing condition. This is compounded by delays in treatment for the accident that is the subject of the lawsuit.

Let's say that you get hurt but don't immediately realize that you have a very bad shoulder as a result of an accident. When you do realize that your shoulder is bothering you, you should inform your medical provider. Hopefully, in the followups, you tell your primary care physician about it as well as any specialist. If you don't, and there is this dreaded "gap" in treatment, it certainly will be an issue the insurance company will raise. So, proximity in time to the accident remains one of the most important things about treating. Otherwise, your case will be contested on what's known as "causality." Again, be aware that these problems are magnified if a pre-existing medical condition is involved.

Some injuries just don't manifest themselves right away. That can be explained. Nonetheless, it is best to operate on the idea that the sooner you realize there is a problem, the sooner you should call its attention to the medical provider. In the case of very severe injuries, it will almost always be very obvious from the outset. But here I am focusing on injuries, some of which turn out to be very serious, where they surface later in time.

Keep a Diary or Journal of Events and Medical Treatment

It is always advisable for clients to keep a diary or a journal. It needn't be as extensive as some very studious clients will make it. It is something just to remind the client of what their condition was months or years before. Let's say your deposition is taken a year after the accident, or even more, the presence of a diary will allow for the appropriate reflection.

One of the most important things in obtaining legal recovery, especially big money recovery, is what the permanent condition will be. Thus, I often say that it is not so much how badly you feel at a closed-end period of time, even if that pain was quite intense. However, you do need to recall, you do need to refresh yourself as to how bad your condition was. Focusing on the early days, the acute phase, isn't mutually exclusive with a long-term picture.

If your permanent injury is your shoulder, it will be important to reacquaint yourself with how your shoulder felt in those first several months after the injury. A diary or journal helps a client refresh his or her recollection, particularly for something like a deposition, but it also helps the attorney to understand the injury. That will enhance the attorney's preparation for mediation or for trial. A diary or a journal is a wonderful thing for you and your lawyer to have.

Why Is A Doctor's Evaluation Crucial To A Personal Injury Case?

Doctor's evaluations of people who have suffered accidents are often the single most important factor in obtaining a high settlement or verdict. Without those evaluations, we are only speculating as to someone's future condition. There is a time and place for lay testimony. In contrast, opinions, conclusions and prognostications (as opposed to descriptions of how someone is feeling) is the province of the medical professional. The appropriate objection to a lay opinion or lay conclusion is that such witness is "not competent" to testify to such matters. We know that the conclusion must come from the doctor but how do we best present that opinion?

Furthermore, in the likely event that we need a prognosis, how do we go about getting that opinion?

A board certified doctor is the individual who is the most logical to speak on these matters. A doctor who is not board certified may be competent to testify but would not be the most persuasive witness. The standard to which the doctor renders opinions on causality (the connection of the accident to the injury), diagnosis, and prognosis is "to a reasonable degree of medical certainty." That is the "tagline" of such questions.

An interesting wrinkle in all of this comes in the circumstance where you ask the doctor to give an opinion as to the injured party's long term prognosis. Again, that prognosis must be "to a reasonable degree of medical certainty." We are talking about civil cases, so the standard for evidentiary proof is "more probable than not." It is not to a reasonable doubt.

Sometimes, I have seen the civil standard compared to a 51% likelihood. Take the following hypothetical: an individual has been injured in an accident and suffers a fracture of a bone. That individual may ultimately develop (and assuming for this discussion has not yet developed) post-traumatic arthritis. However, the doctor may find that the likelihood of post-traumatic arthritis at some point in the future is in the statistical realm of 40%. That is not more probable than not. Am I therefore precluded from obtaining that testimony? After all, it is not to a 51% probability. The answer is no, I am not. The proper way to elicit such a conclusion from the medical expert is whether my client is at "an increased risk of developing that condition."

In the above example, a person's risk may go from 3%, the general population risk, to 40% because of having had the accident. As scientists say, the relative risk is greatly enhanced. In no way should the standard of "more probable than not" preclude this evidence -- evidence which is very significant in determining the value of a personal injury case. Remember, after all, that the big money is paid for the long-term effects of injuries.

WHO IS AN EXPERT?

The distinction between expert witnesses and lay witnesses, as defined by the Federal Rules of Evidence and/or the Massachusetts Guide to Evidence is far more complicated than most people realize. Despite their typical presentation on television, experts are not always doctors, scientists, or professors. As Rule and Guide 702 states, an expert can testify based on the expert's own scientific, technical or other specialized knowledge. Given the last clause, an expert is not confined to a specific set of professional qualifications. For example, an expert can be a baseball player who has played and/or coached at a high level and is able to use his knowledge of the game to clarify a material fact of the case for the jury. As demonstrated by Marisa Tomei's character in the 1992 movie, My Cousin Vinny, an expert can be someone whose knowledge is obtained from a specialized hobby, such as restoring old cars as long as the person can prove that he or she has the knowledge required to testify to the particular subject matter and can assist the jury.

Of course, on the flip-side, Rule 701 confines the testimony of a lay witness to that witness's own perception of a fact or set of facts at issue. That witness will not be allowed to use scientific, technical or specialized knowledge to speculate on these facts. Put more simply, lay witnesses can only report something that they have perceived by using their five senses, whereas expert witnesses typically do not perceive facts firsthand, but instead offer an informed opinion as to a material element of the case or help to clarify certain technical elements of the case for the jury.

By the way, what constitutes an appropriate basis for an opinion is the object of much focus by the appellate courts, state and federal. An opinion must be based upon reliable principles and methods. See Guide to Massachusetts Evidence, Section 702; See also Commonwealth v. Lanigan, 419 Mass. 15, 24-27 (1994).

WHY SHOULD YOU HIRE EXPERTS FOR YOUR PERSONAL INJURY CASE?

I have a very strong philosophy about experts. This philosophy is that the attorney preparing the case should spare no expense, or at least not let money be a dissuading factor. There are two types of experts, liability experts and damages experts. Liability experts might be the engineer, an accident reconstructionist, a human factors specialist, and so on.

The damages experts are the medical professionals and medical doctors. They can be the treating physicians or they can be medical personnel who have evaluated the client for purposes of the case. Moreover, they can belong to several different disciplines. For example, in a head injury case, neurologists, radiologists, neuropsychologists, life care planners, vocational rehabilitation experts, and economists can be used. You could have a whole panoply of experts on just the damages aspects.

These are in addition to the experts that you could have on liability. My all-time total of both liability and damages experts was ten but that didn't mean that I called all ten at trial. Far from it. In the trial, you aren't obligated to call most of them.

Because trials, at least civil trials, are not supposed to be a surprise, you are expected to provide the other side with your experts' reports. The same requirement applies to the other side. Therefore, I take the defense's experts' depositions armed with enough information. The deposition of the expert gives me more information than is contained in the report, all of which means that if and when the case is tried, I will hopefully do a very effective cross-examination of the expert.

The above preparation is very expensive. Unbelievably so. Because your attorney will be paying very good money to hire, prepare, and take testimony of experts (and to take the deposition of opposing experts), make sure, therefore, when hiring a lawyer for a major case, you have an understanding of their willingness to incur major expenses. I never mind laying out thousands of dollars, often tens of thousands of dollars, because that is how the case will result in the best recovery. I often say to clients that "if you want to dance, you have to pay the fiddler." They get it. Unfortunately, I have seen that many lawyers are unwilling to take on such a large financial commitment and the clients suffer.

Furthermore, my philosophy is that I won't ask a client to advance the costs of litigation. Instead, my firm will advance the costs of the litigation. In the extremely unlikely situation where there is no recovery, I am not obliged to ask the client to reimburse me or my firm for expert witnesses or for actually any expenses. And I won't. Never in 35 years have I asked a client where there has been an unsuccessful result to pay me back for what I paid out. Rather, to me it is viewed as a business expense. Fortunately, it's less than 1% of the time that there haven't been recovery. I say "fortunately" because it means my client got a recovery in thousands of cases. If the case is resolved successfully, as almost all of them are, I will then get the fee and be reimbursed for reasonable expenses and disbursements. These will include expert fees, a considerable expense. But these expenses are all taken on because that is how to get the best recovery.

The advantage to my approach is that the client will go to sleep at night during the pendency of the action and not worry about having to pay experts or other expenses. If, God forbid, nothing comes of the case, they will be not be out-of-pocket anything. The advantage is that I can have a very expansive view of who I should hire. It allows me to prepare a case on the opposite of a shoestring budget. That's because if you prepare cases on shoestring budgets, you typically will get a shoestring result.

REASONS WHY YOU SHOULD NOT CHOOSE OPTION OF PRE-SETTLEMENT FUNDING

Paying bills after a major accident is a very difficult problem for most people. There are some limited first-party benefits, but they exist mostly for auto accident victims. Furthermore, they will not last a very long time. In other types of accidents, there are no first-party benefits at all. Into this breach comes pre-settlement finance companies.

You will find no shortage of companies that offer to loan you money on your case. In fact, I have seen them increasingly used in recent years. Having an injury can be a time-consuming, stressful and money-sapping process, especially if the client is out of work. Thus it is no surprise that businesses have been created with the idea of advancing money to injured people. Of course, these companies are in business so they fully expect to get that money back plus interest and fees. It's the "plus interest and fees" that need close examination.

The funding companies will tell you all the right things: an accident is not your fault, you're probably struggling to pay your bills, and if you settle your case soon, you may not get full value on the case. I do not disagree with any of those three statements. The accident was not your fault, the litigation process can be a time-consuming process, and you may settle or "undersettle" your case if you need money quickly.

All true. But nowhere is the old adage that “there is no such thing as a free lunch” more correct than here. Believe me, where these companies are concerned, nothing could be truer than that adage. If you go on their websites, you might not have a sense of what is in store for you. If you’ve taken one of these loans rest assured that when your case finishes, the situation will not be pretty; in fact, it will be downright ugly. I do not mean to disparage the whole industry but I think anybody who is contemplating such a contractual relationship with a funding company should be fully aware of the consequences. The websites don't highlight the very extreme, very prohibitive costs you will have to pay upon the successful completion of your lawsuit.

I, as the attorney, never sign the pre-settlement contracts nor do I encourage my clients to go out and get pre-settlement funding. But inevitably over the last several years, some clients have. The interest rates are exorbitant; every month they go up. I am reminded of what Ben Franklin said on compounding interest and it applies here, "money makes money". Well, being indebted on money means you will be even more indebted as time passes. Actually, the whole notion of compounding means the longer you have the debt, the more interest you will incur. Partly, this arises because of interest on the interest. In the situation of pre-settlement funding, the concept of interest on interest creates a harsh and often unexpected result.

Please note that I have not even addressed the application fees or the processing fees that these companies impose.

The most important thing that you need to be sensitive to at the outset is that the interest rates and all other fees will shock you. Be fully aware of them before you engage in any such contract.

Please keep in mind that I am not talking about structured settlements. Those are a horse of a completely different color. Structured settlements come into play when the client chooses not to have the money in one payment, that is in one lump sum, but instead chooses to have a payout over time. That concept of a structured settlement is a very different proposition than pre-settlement funding because in the former your case has resolved while in the latter you are paying a company to take a chance, an expensive chance, on your case. You want your attorney to protect you. I take that mission seriously and, accordingly, I say to my client that he/she should borrow money from another source. Presumably, a friend, a family member or another source will not impose such draconian interest rates and fees. Tap into those, if at all possible.

WHAT IS MEDIATION?

One of the best tools in a personal injury lawyer's arsenal is mediation. Mediation is a form of alternative dispute resolution. Mediation is a voluntary process and non-binding. It is voluntary in the sense that both parties have to agree to attend. It is not final and binding as in the case of arbitration, yet another form of alternative dispute resolution. Rather, in mediation the two sides are brought together by a neutral third person, often but not necessarily a retired judge, who attempts to effectuate a settlement.

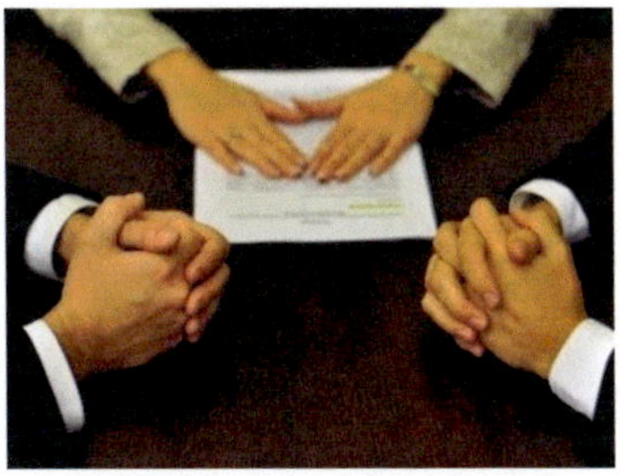

Most major cases are mediated. They can be brought to mediation at any point: before suit is filed, during the litigation, or on the eve of trial. I have seen an evolution in the effectiveness of mediation. When they started to occur with some frequency, approximately 25 years ago, I did not see the success that I have seen over, say, the last decade. (Success is defined as having a case that resolves as a result of the mediation process.) Many mediators will boast a success rate approaching, or even exceeding, 90%.

The people present at the mediation are the opposing lawyers, insurance claims people and the client. The attorney makes the presentation and the client will usually not be asked to say anything. It is quite different from a trial. Indeed, there are no rules of evidence, no one is sworn in and the process is a lot less formal than a trial. But looks can be deceiving. While the process does not have the grandeur or formality of a trial, the result is very meaningful. If the mediation is successful, it will allow for the injured party to receive compensation.

After short introductory remarks by the mediator, the process starts with a presentation by me, the plaintiff's attorney. (I will discuss the seriousness with which I approach a mediation in the next chapter.) The defendant then makes its presentation. After that, the parties are separated, usually for the entire mediation. I sit with my clients while the defense attorney and insurance company representatives are placed in another room. The actual defendants, as opposed to the insurance company representatives, are almost never there. Throughout the course of the morning and afternoon, the mediator engages in "shuttle diplomacy," going back and forth between the two rooms, all the while exchanging settlement figures. If the process works according to form, at the end of the day, or perhaps by telephone in a few weeks, the case is resolved.

As I say, years ago I was a skeptic where mediation was concerned. After all, the process is only as good as the money the insurance company brings to the table. Fortunately, I am seeing many instances where they are bringing a proper amount of money.

What Makes For An Effective Mediation In A Personal Injury Case?

Hopefully, in the last chapter I established the wisdom of going to a mediation. This chapter will address how I, as your attorney, believe the mediation should be approached. The mediation is done in a private office, not in a courtroom. It is nevertheless adversarial, although politely so. There can be more than ten people present. Thus, there may be several representatives for several parties.

As much as I say it is an informal process -- without the rules of evidence, without testimony, without a judge or jury -- it starts to feel very important. I am cognizant of that feeling to remind myself how important it is to prepare. That is why I say, "There is no substitute for preparation, preparation, preparation." The stakes are as high as in a courtroom because at the end of the day you are seeking full compensation for your injured client. I enjoy the opportunity to give my overview of the case at the outset of the mediation. I will never approach a mediation in a casual way. My presentation, consisting of approximately twenty minutes, will rely upon excerpts from depositions, medical records and, of course, demonstrative evidence. My effort and seriousness of purpose is there to give insight as to how the accident happened and to depict the injuries in a clear and potentially dramatic way.

At the end of the presentation, I want the defense, the attorneys, and insurance companies for whom the lawyers work, to know that if this case were to go to trial, it would be ready and it would be strenuously presented. I do not tend to hold back in a mediation and there are strategic reasons to "let it all out." The foremost reason is that this is your chance to show the other side, as well as the mediator, how strong a case you have. Sometimes, gaps in the other side's case are not apparent or have not been pointed out during depositions, for example. This is the time to present a summation and to show, for example, that there have been contradictory theories put forth by the adversary. Some plaintiff's lawyers may feel that they are revealing too much. I, on the other hand, would rather put my best foot forward and, hopefully, cause the other side to assess (or reassess) my case and to question themselves on whether they have a defensible case.

The purpose of the mediator's "shuttle diplomacy" is to begin the process of exchanging numbers in an effort to come to a settlement figure. In reaching that settlement, it helps if the plaintiff knows what he or she can put in his pocket, after the payment of Medicare, private health, or worker's compensation liens, as will often be the case. It may not be possible to know the exact number but if that is a sticking point, the case need not settle on the day of the mediation. It is hoped, however, that the process may lead to a settled case. That hope doesn't reveal weakness; it reveals a realistic assessment of what is best for your client.

WHAT ARE THE MOST DIFFICULT TYPES OF PERSONAL INJURY CLAIMS?

When talking about head injuries or brain injuries, you will often hear of the term, the silent epidemic. Even though the client may look fine and may seemingly act fine, something is going on with them. One reason is that the victim compensates for these new deficits and/or they cover up for their new-found deficiencies. From medical science we know the reality: that something is not quite right. In the case of a brain injury, oftentimes the CT scan and/or the MRI will be negative, a good finding meaning nothing is wrong on those studies or at least it would so appear. However, a lot of scratching beneath the surface will uncover that the client is having difficulty. It is up to the lawyer to prove the brain injury despite the CT scan and MRI results showing no abnormality. This is doable but it requires effort and a familiarity with what to look for and where to look.

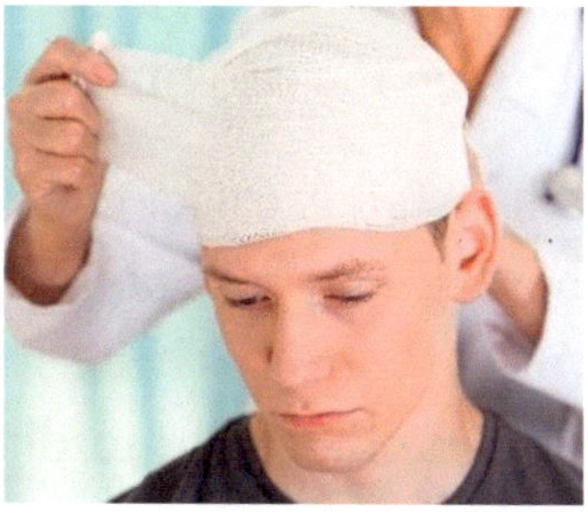

In spite of a skeptical insurance company, these cases can indeed be proven; in other words, you can prove a head injury in the absence of CT scan findings or MRI findings. How? You do it through lay testimony, you do it through family members and co-workers, you do it from school records, you do it from employer evaluations, you do it from the client himself/herself, you do it through neuropsychologists, you do it through psychiatrists or psychologists, so on and so forth. There is therefore a mix of lay and expert witnesses. The key point to remember, as with any personal injury case, is the before and after. You must illustrate in a vivid way the differences in the client between the two time periods.

It is certainly easier to prove a significant head injury where there has been an abnormal finding such as in a CT scan or MRI. If there has been an intracranial bleed, then it's easier for the other side to digest the fact that there is a head injury. Even in those cases where there has been that kind of a finding, where the study has shown something is wrong, there will be a temptation on the other side to say it's not that bad. They will say that things have resolved. But the serious lawyer is always endeavoring to show that the injury remains significant: it has affected the person in every facet of his or her life, including at home, at school, at work, recreationally and so forth.

I am increasingly handling head injuries. I like the science. Moreover for one who never particularly liked biology, I am drawn to the whole panoply of injuries such as back and neck injuries, where the insurers have a certain skepticism. In case of a significant injury, such as a broken neck or broken back, you should be able to overcome the skepticism we often see in a soft tissue case.

Injuries to joints such as the ankle, shoulder, wrist, knee, and hip can present challenges. As we age, we start having problems in these areas. Even though somebody will have a significant break in one of those areas as a result of the accident, they may have had problems there beforehand. That gets into the whole pre-existing condition phenomenon.

Consider a slight variation of the pre-existing situation where the client had a problem but it was not symptomatic until the accident. Take the example of a spine injury, where somebody had some sort of spinal condition, such as a lot of degeneration, but it didn't bother them until they had their injury. In that instance, the law is very helpful because it says that this is a triggering of an otherwise dormant, silent condition. This is not an exacerbation. That is something that should be fully compensable because it did not give the person any problem, any symptomatology, before but it gives them problems now. Therefore, it's a little different from the exacerbation situation. But whether it is an exacerbation or the triggering of a pre-existing asymptomatic condition, an insurance company will seek to reduce their payment. It is the job of a savvy lawyer, one who knows the law and the anatomy, to give the other side pause.

What Makes Premises Liability Cases Different And More Challenging?

One thing to understand about personal injury cases is that insurers will contend that people don't have these accidents if they are watching where they are going. If they had the accident, the insurance company will automatically declare that the client wasn't being careful. There is also the old viewpoint that

anytime there is an accident, the victim was comparatively negligent. What is the effect of comparative negligence? The insurer is looking to reduce the payout because of that specter.

I have had excellent results on premises liability cases. Perhaps the defect was latent. Latent or hidden defects are things that even in the exercise of the highest level of care, the victim would not be able to uncover. If the defect is latent, at a minimum, the defendant has a duty to warn those who might encounter it. Of course, the better practice is to remedy it. Was the client acting reasonably? This is the standard on both the defendant and the plaintiff. This is all that can be expected of a person in the eyes of the law.

Taking another example, one which comes up decade after decade, is stairway accidents. The insurer will argue that the plaintiff used that same stairway without incident before the subject accident. The insurance company will also try to say that other people walked on that stairway and none of them had an accident. I have made numerous arguments before Superior Court judges in the state courts of Massachusetts that such evidence of non-accidents to the client or to others should not come into play. In making that argument, I cite the philosophy espoused by a judge of the Federal Court, formerly of the state court, and a foremost lecturer on evidence, who says that we are all kind of self-sufficient, autonomous and go our own way. Therefore, even if someone had an accident, he argues, he/she might not complain. Thus, there is no way to know whether there was truly an absence of accidents. Judges seem to have no hard and fast rule on this issue but I will certainly make the argument to attempt to exclude this evidence.

Then there is the transitory condition in premises liability cases. Think banana peel. How long was it there before your client fell? Was it close to where an employee was stationed? Did the defendant or its employees have actual notice of the object? Even better, can you prove that one of the employees caused it to be there? If so, then you probably don't have to show how long it was present. My firm faces these circumstances in supermarket cases, among others, and we have been very successful in handling them. In one instance, we obtained millions of dollars when the store manager admitted in a deposition that "sure, we could have done better." The transitory condition of a spilled drink in one of the aisles was deemed to have been there long enough such that it should have been cleaned up or properly warned of, if the supermarket's employees were acting with due care. In that instance, the presence of only one cone was admitted by the supermarket not to be a sufficient warning. We had the best of all worlds in the case: the placement of a single cone proved actual notice on the part of the supermarket and yet its remedy was half-hearted.

Obstacles To Getting The Compensation You Deserve

The three primary obstacles to getting the compensation you deserve are insufficient insurance, comparative negligence, and pre-existing conditions.

A central feature of car accident cases is insurance law. The sad fact is, regardless of how badly someone is hurt, if there isn't much insurance coverage on the offending vehicle or the offending driver, then the client runs a real risk of being undercompensated.

In these cases, something can be done by a consumer or purchaser of insurance to mitigate the harshness of limited insurance coverage. This is called bodily injury coverage by an uninsured vehicle or an underinsured vehicle. They are under Parts 3 and 12 of your Coverage Selection Page. The problem is that uninsured or underinsured coverage will cost a little bit more. However, it's true that it's the only kind of coverage that you can get to protect yourself and your family. It will protect you and household members if they are in a car, someone else's car, are a pedestrian or a bicyclist.

Oftentimes, clients don't have enough coverage under Part 3 and Part 12 of the Massachusetts Auto Policy. If they are injured by the negligence of another driver, and the insurance limits are minimal on their own (the client's) vehicle, the client will not have access to their own policy for additional coverage. That's very unfortunate because the premium for this coverage is not all that high. If you have coverage under those sections, accessing it will not cause your insurer to surcharge you. It is considered first party coverage that comes into play because of the negligence of a third party. It's a simple and relatively inexpensive way of protecting yourself and your household members. I can't tell you the number of times that I have had a client tell me that they have "full insurance" only to have them disappointed when we look at the Coverage Selection Page. It is especially troubling to see limited coverage for Parts 3 and 12 on a client who has a lot of insurance for Part 5. Part 5 covers bodily injury to others. It makes the failure to have matching limits on Parts 3 and 12 all the more vexing. Frankly, it is a mistake on the part of the insurance agent to allow this situation.

Having covered insurance, let's focus on the doctrine of comparative negligence. It comes into play in all types of tort cases, including products liability (where negligence is alleged and not in warranty cases), premises liability, and auto cases. In other words, if somebody falls or somebody is using something improperly, there is an argument by the defense that they were not as careful as they should have been. Since 1973, Massachusetts has had what is called a comparative negligence statute. That certainly is an improvement over what the law was before, which stated that if you were at all at fault, you couldn't recover. Now, we have a form of comparative negligence that says if you are 50% or less negligent, you will recover, although your damages will be reduced by the percentage that you were negligent.

You should keep in mind that even with the relatively indulgent and kind comparative negligence statute (at least compared to its predecessor of contributory negligence), if you are 51% or more negligent, you will not recover anything. A finding of 51% comparative negligence precludes or bars recovery. Other states, such as Florida, where I am admitted to practice, have a pure comparative negligence doctrine. It allows for recovery even where the person suing is 99% negligent, though the damages are reduced by the percentage of comparative negligence. We are not as indulgent in Massachusetts but I am certainly happy to be practicing now rather than before 1973, when what existed was the rigid doctrine of contributory negligence, a complete bar to recovery.

Thus, when dealing with a situation where somebody is 50% or less negligent, you know that they will recover something, albeit a reduced amount. That is another obstacle that has to be brought to the would-be plaintiff's attention. There are many arguments that insurance companies or defense lawyers can use to try to negate any recovery at all. The first one is quite obvious where they say, "Well, this person got hurt but the condition was open and obvious." Indeed those terms, open and obvious, are known even to the new practitioners, both plaintiff and defense lawyers. Interestingly, a careful reading of the case law in Massachusetts is that open and obvious is only a defense to the doctrine of failure to warn. Therefore, it is often overused by defense lawyers. Once again, a proper understanding of Massachusetts' tort law, personal injury law, will allow the competent practitioner to defeat a defense argument.

Another obstacle to recovery, or a full recovery, is when a case involves pre-existing conditions. When people get to a certain stage in life, it seems incredibly common that they have problems with the same part of the body or the same condition which they have hurt in the subject accident. You will hear of the term “degeneration.”

The careful plaintiff's lawyer argues that the law is very clear that the defendant takes the plaintiff as he or she finds them. That means if somebody is more prone or more apt to have an injury, the law doesn't exonerate the tortfeasor. The law does say that the defendant tortfeasor must pay only for the exacerbation or aggravation of that injury. However, the notion among practitioners for years on the other side, i.e. the defense practitioners, is that juries are suspicious of anyone who had a prior condition involving the same part of the body or anatomy that is the subject of the suit. The old-style lawyers maintain that in spite of what the legal principle is, which is that you take the plaintiff as you find him, jurors will not be inclined to compensate.

The view of the defense practitioners, that you'll never get money on those cases, is just not true. In fact, you do. I have gotten a lot of money for a lot of people who have had pre-existing conditions. However, it is something with which your lawyer will have to contend. It is said that when you file a personal injury suit, you open up your life to scrutiny. That is true. But, if in the process it is learned that you had a problem with the same part of the body that is in issue in the lawsuit, don't despair.

As we have also discussed, discovery is a major part of civil cases and it is designed to ward off surprise. Thus the adversary can seek to obtain medical records that go back years, many years before the accident. Other types of discovery will pertain to liability factors. Your personal injury lawyer must be prepared for a ride that isn't always smooth. We are, after all, dealing with real life situations that are seldom 100% cut and dried.

Things That Insurance Companies Look For To Debunk Your Case

Insurance companies love to debunk a case. Sometimes, they will find illegitimate reasons and sometimes legitimate reasons. You know from reading this book that pre-existing conditions are a fertile ground for them. They love to mine the pre-existing condition phenomenon. They think bureaucratically. "Oh, pre-existing condition. That's on our checklist." Yes, we've discussed that by now. But to really get a sense of their mindset consider some of their other arguments from their arsenal to have a sense of the disingenuous nature of the other side.

In defending a case of scarring, an insurance company will say about scarring on a young boy, "Well, it's on a boy, it's not on a girl." Then if that same scar occurs on a girl, they are apt to say, "Oh, scarring whether on a boy or girl doesn't matter." That's their mentality.

Although many insurance company representatives are honest, decent people, that doesn't mean you should let your guard down. A good attorney will often say to their clients before a deposition, "Be prepared for the wolf in sheep's clothing." Another of my catechisms is, "Be polite but firm." An opposing attorney can come in and ask you questions in a very nice, seemingly sympathetic way, but you should treat them as a wolf because they want to save their side money. That's their job. They may be scrupulous and careful and decent people, but their job is 180 degrees different from your attorney's job. Your attorney's job is to get his/her client the most money. The adversary's job is to get the insurance company to save the most money. It may all be litigated in a very polite fashion but the high stakes remain.

I use the golden rule, "If they are nice, you be nice." My mantra of being "polite but firm" suggests that you want to be mindful of the fact that the other side is concerned with how you present yourself. Hence: be polite. But you don't want to be cajoled, intimidated or seduced into saying something that is not the case. You don't want to say that you've fully recovered if, in fact, you haven't fully recovered. Hence: be firm.

The balance found in my "polite but firm" principle is a good basis on which the client, and I, should proceed.

How Can You Get A Lot Of Money At A Personal Injury Trial - the lawyer uses the evidence to advantage

Rules of evidence are like a chess game. Getting in favorable evidence and keeping unfavorable evidence out are the touchstone of trial work. Many attorneys shake their heads when they don't quite understand what's going on. Since I know hearsay, I am very confident in the hurly burly of objecting and the like. Of course, I should be very comfortable with evidentiary principles because I studied hearsay for about four hours each night while in law school. I've been speaking about this part of legal work, arguing about it, and commenting about it for close to 40 years, 35 years in practice and in the second and third years of law school.

If there is a tricky evidentiary point, it could be raised in what's called a "motion in limine," which is Latin for "in advance" of trial. It could also be discussed at sidebar where the plaintiff's lawyer and the defendant's lawyer come up to the side of the judge's bench, out of the hearing of the jury, and argue the point. I've been so motivated and animated during these discussions that I've been told by the court reporter to modulate my voice and not to bring my hand down on the judge's bench.

Yes, I bring passion to these evidentiary arguments. Feeling strongly about these issues allows me to give verbatim statements of doctrines, for example, "Hearsay is an out of court statement offered to prove the truth of the matter asserted." It cannot come in evidence unless there are exceptions. There are so many different layers of hearsay. Something could be seemingly hearsay but it might be offered for what's called a non-hearsay purpose or it could indeed be hearsay but fall into an exception.

There are numerous ways to approach evidentiary issues but you really need a lawyer grounded in it. Consider, for example, the record-setting boiler verdict I was privileged to obtain. I was confronted with an OSHA investigation that faulted my client's employer. Because of worker's compensation immunity from suit, the employer wasn't a defendant. I knew that the introduction of that OSHA conclusion would be fatal to my case because it would allow the jury to say that the employer, not the entity being sued, was at fault. (The OSHA findings didn't blame the parties who were being sued nor the parties who prepared the boiler at this condominium complex.) Therefore, I had to keep that conclusion and opinion out. Happily, the defense-oriented judge sided with me in my motion in limine (motion in advance of trial) and kept that potentially very harmful conclusion out. However, there is case law in Massachusetts that says while the opinions and conclusions can't come in evidence, the facts and observations made by an investigator can. Those factual findings from the OSHA report were used by me to great effect. Thus, I got the best of all worlds: I kept out the bad conclusion and got in the good factual findings.

Had I not known about a particular Massachusetts case from 1980, Julian v. Randazzo, 380 Mass. 391 that controlled this situation where facts and observations come in as opposed to conclusions and opinions, the result would likely have been different. Also note that the Rules of Evidence for the Federal Court would have allowed this dreadful report to be in evidence in all respects, even the conclusion. Accordingly, choosing the forum for your case is no small matter for your lawyer.

Misconceptions That People Have About Personal Injury Cases

The biggest misconception regarding personal injury cases is the tendency for people to think of the legal process playing out as it is depicted on TV. TV gives people the impression that cases will resolve very quickly, maybe in the hour-long TV episode or, if it's a miniseries, maybe over a couple of episodes. It doesn't work that way. Having said that, personal injury cases are processed in a much quicker way than they were several years ago.

Injuries have to mature, so to speak. Sometimes, you will see it referred to as a maximum medical result. Whether we call it mature or maximum medical result, the client has to reach that stage. If the case continues long enough, the attorney may also have to get the appropriate deposition testimony from a physician(s) who will say what the reasonably expected future is for the client. In other words, the doctor will have to testify to the client's ongoing symptoms and effects from the injuries. Even though I am describing a case where there are permanent injuries, at some point medical professionals will be able to say to a reasonable degree of medical certainty what the future holds for the client. Getting to that stage can take a while, even though you don't have to wait for the injury to stop having effects.

Once that stage is reached, your lawyer has to get a final narrative from at least one doctor. If you need to have the doctor provide a deposition, arranging for the testimony will take an additional amount of time. Once you have those conclusions and/or testimony, and assuming they are to a reasonable degree of medical certainty, you are ready to negotiate with the insurance company. Increasingly, insurance companies seek to mediate cases, as we have learned.

Another misconception comes in the auto claims cases, about compensation levels or potential compensation levels. The compensation is often dependent upon the amount of insurance coverage. We have discussed this and it bears repeating: regardless of how seriously injured a person is, or even if killed, so much depends on the existence of proper insurance. Regrettably, it is a very difficult process to get anything beyond that. You cannot get blood out of a stone. If a driver has the minimum in coverage or just a little bit more than the minimum, and that underinsured driver has no assets (as is almost always the case), the deserving client will be out of luck absent underinsurance. Hopefully, as discussed, underinsurance was obtained by the client. If not, the lawyer cannot be a magician and produce coverage that doesn't exist.

These are factors beyond the best lawyers' control that will limit the amount of the award. Again, in commercial contexts or in premises liability cases, which have sufficient insurance, this should not be a problem.

Another misconception is that people think, "Well, if I have been hurt and there is insurance, doesn't the insurance exist to pay me?" The truth is, "No, it doesn't." We live in a fault based society. You may have heard of no-fault divorce and you may have heard of no-fault personal injury protection benefits. So-called PIP benefits don't cover pain and suffering. We are in a fault-based society for tort or personal injury cases. Every jurisdiction in this country requires fault to recover for pain and suffering. That is something that needs to be borne in mind.

Taking another example of a worker who was hurt on the job while in the course and scope of his employment, that person is entitled to worker's compensation benefits but they are limited to set amounts. The "comp" insurer pays for lost wages and only a percentage of them. They pay for medical bills. But the worker doesn't recover for pain and suffering unless there is another party, not the employer, who was negligent. Then you can pursue your action for pain and suffering against that non-employer. That is a tort case.

Liens are very common in this day and age. A lien can be in the form of a medical lien from a health insurer who has contracted with you and says in effect: "We have an automatic right to recover the amount we have paid out if you are suing a third-party for negligence. We can recover up to the amount that we paid out but not to exceed your recovery." This leads to a negotiation. There are also liens from worker's compensation carriers on the third-party recovery. Then there are liens that arise automatically by federal or state law. For example, in the case of Medicare, they don't even need to notify you according to statutes and the Code of Federal Regulations. With state programs, settlements have to be "run" through the Department of Revenue for back child support, taxes or medical care.

As Yogi Berra said, "It ain't over till it's over."

Getting Compensation For An Injury Caused By A Dog

Recovery for an injury from a dog depends upon the existence of homeowner's insurance coverage on the owner or keeper of the dog. Any injury that occurs as a result of a dog is compensable. The injury need not be an actual bite but could occur as a result of a bump, a trip, or even if a dog causes you to fall from a bicycle. The law in Massachusetts is M.G.L. c. 140, s. 155, "Liability For Damage Caused By Dog."

The most notable feature of this statute is that the damage need only to have occurred. The applicable standard is strict liability. In comparison, almost all personal injury law requires a showing of negligence to prevail. That is not the case with the dog statute. Your lawyer need only show that the dog was owned or kept by the defendant and that damage occurred as a result of the actions of the dog. As a result, a dog's dangerous propensities are not relevant. Leash laws are likewise not relevant. The statute does include the fact that there will not be recovery if the damage "shall have been occasioned to the body or property of a person, who at the time such damage was sustained, was committing a trespass or other tort, or was teasing, tormenting or abusing such dog." I haven't had a client sue who was found to have been teasing, tormenting or abusing the dog who caused the damage.

Homeowner's insurance will cover the owner or keeper. In recent years, I am noticing that some breeds of dogs are excluded from Homeowner's coverage. They are blacklisted from coverage. If that is the case, hopefully the homeowner did indeed find another insurance company offering coverage which includes that dog.

It seems that most of the dog attack cases that I have encountered are bites. Not only that, many involve facial scarring. To proceed with those cases involves most of the usual work in a personal injury case. At least that work does not include any concern over whether I can establish negligence because the statute speaks very clearly in the plaintiff's favor. If the dog isn't man's best friend, the statute is.

THINGS THAT SURPRISE PEOPLE IN PERSONAL INJURY CASES

One of the biggest surprises is the special verdict form. A jury just doesn't go back and retire to deliberate and say, "How much we are giving this plaintiff?" They have to go through special questions. The first question is, "Was the defendant negligent?" They must answer "Yes" for there to be a recovery. But they also have to answer a second question "Yes" and that is, "Was the negligence a substantial contributing cause of the injuries?" If that second question is answered "No," even though the first question was answered "Yes", there will be no recovery. If the answers to both of the first two questions are "Yes," then the jury will get to comparative negligence and so forth. Getting a recovery is not quite as straightforward a matter as we'd like.

I will not discuss liens in this chapter (see the last chapter) but they do indeed surprise clients when they hear about them for the first time. I understand. I left law school thinking a lien pertained to an encumbrance on property, i.e. a mortgage. The lien concept, harsh as it is, has a broader impact than in real estate.

The likelihood of a trial or non-likelihood surprises clients. See the next chapter.

Questions That Personal Injury Lawyers Are Frequently Asked

There are several questions that personal injury lawyers are frequently asked. Some of them are as follows:

Will My Case Go to Trial or Settle?

One of the most common questions is whether a client's case will be tried or settled. Contrary to what we see on TV, most cases settle before trial. However, even if the case is settled, a lawsuit may have been filed and discovery will have taken place. Your case could go almost to the point of a trial. There are many opportunities for settling prior to entering the courtroom, and even thereafter. This is why mediation has become an often used tool and most litigators will consider it as an option. What I said earlier bears repeating: cases that are prepared for trial are settled, while cases that are prepared for settling are tried. It is important to make sure your lawyer is fully prepared. As the client, you have the right to expect this.

What Is a Major Factor in a Settlement?

A recent Boston Globe article described a plaintiff in a significant lawsuit who was awarded $580,000 but netted virtually nothing after the deduction of fees, medical expenses and medical liens. We must revisit liens because they have taken on an outsized position in cases. Years ago, I blogged about a "lien" being not necessarily "lean." See www.feinbergalban.com/blogs. There is no question that liens can lead to very unfortunate results. Liens, such as those in a self-funded ERISA plan, do not require the lien-holder to lower or reduce the health plan's lien. In fact, the United States Supreme Court in a recent case sadly upheld the right of the ERISA plan to reimbursement from a third party recovery even where the plaintiff would NET NOTHING. US Airways v. James E. McCutchen 569 U.S. (2013). Arguments raising equitable doctrines were rejected because of relevant contract provisions. The Supreme Court found that the agreement — calling for full reimbursement to the plan — and not equitable principles provides the measure of relief.

The Supreme Court discussed the policy behind what seems to be a draconian result. I endeavor to make sure that my clients do not walk away empty-handed. Sometimes the lawyer has to act equitably, even if the lien-holder doesn't.

What Should I Know About Scarring in a Personal Injury Case?

My clients should keep in mind two "Ps": Pictures and Prognostication. Pictures at the time the scar was sustained and pictures of the scarring after some time has passed are very important for obvious reasons.

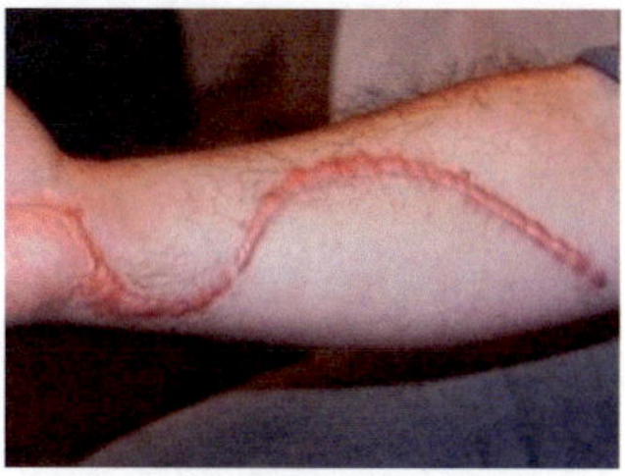

Unfortunately, this means that the client will need to have taken pictures of the scarring within days of the accident. Pictures taken immediately, when the injury is in its "acute" stage, are often graphic and should be in the plaintiff lawyer's arsenal for effective representation. (This doesn't really contradict my heavy focus on the long term effects of an injury.) If there is no attorney, however, and if the client has not taken pictures, that will be an opportunity that may be lost. But not necessarily lost because there is yet one more source: the hospital or plastic surgeon with whom the client treated often takes photographs. If cosmetics is involved, increasingly medical providers want to preserve the situation by photographs.

The second P, Prognostication, comes from an expert. As with virtually every personal injury case, you need medical experts to establish causality, prognosis and impairment. In a scarring case, attorneys especially want to determine the permanence of the scar. If the scarring is indeed permanent, they will want to know whether it will get better with time, and, if so, how much better. The salient medical question will be whether the scar has "matured." If so, then the doctors know how it will look in the future.

Insurers will also want to know whether certain surgical procedures are available to improve the condition of the scar. If the answer to that inquiry is yes, then it will be important to know what the fees will be for the surgery. This will include the surgeon's fee, the anesthesiologist's fee and the facility's fee. These are fair questions because they come under the rubric of reasonably anticipated medical costs. The inquiry does not stop there, however. They want to know *how* improved the scar will be by any procedure. This essentially requires a verbal description by the medical expert but it could be enhanced by some sort of physical rendering. In conclusion, a scarring case requires a careful and thorough exploration of the past, the present and the future.

Does the Client's Profile Impact the Value of the Case?

This is a question that attorneys frequently encounter. It is a legitimate and appropriate question for a personal injury client to ask. This part of the book will discuss how credibility is "king". Is the person bringing the lawsuit honest? Is the person reliable? What is the background of the accident victim client? Does he or she have a background that is consistent with hard work? Has he or she been productive before the accident?

The answers to the above questions go a long way into forming the personal biography - or, in today's vernacular, the personal narrative - which will be very much a part of my presentation as your personal injury lawyer.

It makes a difference when you are able to represent honest and likable clients. The other side can discern those qualities quite easily. Further, those qualities help to create a picture of a client who is candid about case specific events: how the accident occurred, their injuries, and any of the facts that are deemed relevant to the case.

As I see it then, the answer to the question in this chapter starts with the client and the client's personal characteristics.

The answer doesn't end there but it is certainly a foundational element in the determination of value.

Without a credible, likeable, and hardworking client it is very hard to obtain sufficient compensation in a serious personal injury case. Partly, that is due to the increased likelihood that a serious case will be resolved further along in the process, i.e. closer to the time of trial. Therefore, there are more opportunities for the defendant to see who the plaintiff is. That can come about from other witnesses who come to a deposition or through records, such as employment files, medical documents, or any other material that may be relevant to the action and relevant to who the plaintiff is.

Will My Attorney Charge Me on a Contingent Basis or on an Hourly Basis?

Another question is whether a personal injury attorney will charge on a contingent basis or on an hourly basis. Feinberg & Alban P.C. takes cases only on a contingent fee basis. This benefits the client because he/she is not expected to pay for the attorney's time. Additionally, the firm does not expect expenses to be reimbursed as they are incurred. We will pay for those expenses and only upon resolving the case favorably will we get our fee and be reimbursed for the expenses. My firm provides you with a listing of the expenses that have occurred. They must be reasonable by the terms of the Contingent Fee Agreement. As stated earlier, in the very few cases in which there has not been a recovery, my firm will not ask the client for reimbursement of the case expenses and, of course, we can't be compensated for our work.

Clients often ask if their share of the recovery is going to be taxed. In the Internal Revenue Code's definition of income, personal injury awards and settlements are excluded. Personal injury cases are not taxable, neither by the federal government nor the state. Congress has carved out a few exceptions to this nice rule for some civil cases - mainly in the field of wrongful termination - but settlements or awards for personal injury are not taxable nor should anyone tell you otherwise. This helpful fact has eluded some seasoned attorneys and not a few accountants.

Will I Get the Recovery Amount in a Lump Sum or Over Time?

Clients frequently ask the question of whether they will get their money in a lump sum or if the recovery will be paid out over time. In some cases, the awards are paid out over time in what is known as a structured settlement. That takes the form of an annuity payment. The best reasons for a structured settlement are that the entire payout, including the interest, are tax free and that payouts over time make being careless with the money much more difficult. The first reason, that the income stream is all tax free, is largely diminished because interest rates are now so low. But the second reason exists and will continue to exist as long as we are dealing with human nature. I don't, however, take a paternalistic attitude by pointing my clients in the direction of a structure; it is truly up to them. There is no requirement to take a settlement in a structure.

What Auto Insurance Coverage Do I Need to Protect Myself in Case of an Accident in Massachusetts?

Automobile insurance will protect you in the event that you are sued for your alleged negligence. There is Compulsory Bodily Injury Coverage under Part 1 but you would be well advised to choose Part 5, Optional Bodily Injury Coverage. There are three reasons for this: Part 5 covers you if you are sued by guest passengers; it covers you out-of-state; and you can buy far more coverage than the compulsory limits that are available under Part 1 of $20,000 per person/$40,000 per accident. However, there are two other coverages that you can select which will protect you and your family as well as guest occupants in some circumstances. Those coverages are Part 3, Bodily Injury Caused By an Uninsured Auto, and Part 12, Bodily Injury Caused By an Underinsured Auto. The bottom line is that you need enough coverage to access those. Limits of $20,000 per person/$40,000 per accident are not enough.

An "uninsured auto" is defined as a hit and run vehicle, a stolen vehicle or if the driver has failed to obtain valid insurance despite the requirements in Massachusetts. Think of the following situation: You are hurt by a car with no insurance and suffer a significant personal injury. If, however, you have opted for the minimum limits under Part 3, you will find that there is barely enough money to pay for medical bills and/or liens, let alone enough money to compensate you.

An "underinsured auto" is defined as an auto where the limits of the at-fault vehicle are not enough to compensate you for your damages. The law allows you to be compensated from your own vehicle's policy in that circumstance. However, you are only able to collect if your limits in Part 12 are more than the limits of the at-fault driver. Think of the following situation: You are hurt as badly as you were in the above paragraph but your limits under Part 12 are so low that they do not exceed the bodily injury limits of the negligent party. In that unhappy circumstance, you will have nowhere to turn for your compensation, including money for pain and suffering.

Should I Give a Statement to an Insurance Company?

The request from the insurance company for a statement raises a few intriguing questions. First, is the client obligated to give a statement? If it is a car accident case, the client is obligated to give a statement when seeking so-called first party benefits, i.e. PIP (Personal Injury Protection). The authority for this is contained in the auto insurance policy. It states that in the event a person is seeking payment under certain provisions of the policy, the insurance company has the right to take an examination under oath. However, if attorneys are dealing with a so-called third party insurer, the client does not have to give a statement. Additionally, there is a right to decline to give a statement in other types of personal injury cases, i.e. non-auto cases.

In a third-party auto case, premises case, or a products case a statement is optional. As a matter of tactics, should the lawyer advise the client to agree to give a statement in those circumstances? Usually the answer is no, because you would be giving the opposition the opportunity to question a client prior to litigation, and once litigation begins, that other side will have an automatic right to take the deposition of that party. This will enable the adversary to be educated in ways that would not have been possible if the client had not given the statement before the lawsuit began.

In certain circumstances, attorneys allow for clients to give statements before a case is in suit. There are two considerations which guide them. The first is whether the client makes a good appearance and can narrate in a coherent way how the accident occurred. The second principle to keep in mind is the nature of how it is conducted by the other side. Can it be informal such as merely an interview? If not an interview, will it be a handwritten statement which is then signed by the client? In some limited cases, the attorney might agree to that. In almost no event should the attorney agree to a recorded interview.

Also, if a client hopes for a quick resolution, the attorney may be more inclined to agree to the client's giving a statement. The lawyer must sit down with the client to discuss the best approach given the circumstances. He/She will ask: are you willing to give the other side two bites of the apple - a statement and then a deposition?

What to Look for When You Hire an Attorney?

The qualities and characteristics that you look for when hiring an injury attorney are fairly obvious. You want someone who is familiar with the law, has experience, and someone with whom you have a comfort level. On the last point, the attorney-client relationship should be a very strong one as you are working closely together and most likely the relationship will be for more than a year. In fact, in the most serious personal injury cases you will be working together for

a couple of years, in large part because the injury will not be at a medical end point until that time.

There should be a flow of communication between you and the attorney. Sometimes the flow will be with key staff members of the law firm. This is not to say that the attorney's role is diminished but only to point out that the day-to-day tasks of getting medical records and the like are typically handled by paralegals. But you will still have a flow of communication with the lawyer. You want to make him or her aware of any developments on liability, including the existence of witnesses, and obviously any developments with respect to your injury.

Topics to be included are the ongoing functional limitations, pain level, medication, medical providers and a general discussion of how the activities of daily living have been affected. I often ask clients to provide me with a diary at regular intervals to keep me apprised of these developments. The purpose of a diary is several fold: it will refresh a client's recollection as to how they were feeling at a particular point in time, particularly in the acute stages of the injury; it allows me to get a "real time" sense of how the injuries are unfolding; and allows me to provide an insurer or a defense attorney with meaningful information when they call for the inevitable status update.

You should want your lawyer to be abreast of your situation. However, the purpose is not to ask for the lawyer's input in your medical treatment. It is not appropriate, ethically or tactically, for the lawyer to involve himself or herself in the treatment course of the client. The ethics for that are obvious. But why is it tactically inadvisable? Almost from the first days of my becoming a lawyer, I learned of the defendant's line of inquiry involving how the client found a particular doctor. You can well imagine the dangers of having a lawyer who is seen as the choreographer of the medical treatment. Now, to be clear, asking a client to be evaluated by an eminent physician, a medical doctor who is Board Certified in the specialty involved, is appropriate. But that is a different proposition from an attorney who advises a client to go to one place or another for medical treatment. The attorney should not do that as a matter of ethics or as a matter of tactics. There is no place for the lawyer to insinuate himself in the medical treatment process.

Can I Change Lawyers in a Personal Injury Case?

First a bit of background: the Rules of Professional Responsibility require that a Contingent Fee Agreement "be in writing and signed in duplicate by both the lawyer and the client..." S.J.C. Rule 3:07, Rule 1.5(c). The rule sets out the cases in which a contingent fee is permissible – there must be a res, Latin, for a thing or object, and in this context, a sum of money – and it includes the category of personal injury. Numerous other rules have been added to 1.5(c). These requirements are welcome because the contingent fee contract spells out the rights of the consumer clearly.

Years ago, it was not uncommon to have a client who had discharged another office where no contingent fee agreement had been signed. In more recent years, I have found that the discharged lawyer indeed has had a signed contingent fee agreement. But whatever the scenario, the crucial point for the consumer is that he/she should never pay twice for the cost of pursuing a case. Accordingly, when Feinberg & Alban P.C. takes on a case which has been with another office, it always puts in the fee agreement that its compensation will be reduced by the amount which is owed to the prior attorney. This is the fairest way to resolve what can be a difficult dilemma: it insures that the client will be able to use an attorney with whom he/she is comfortable and yet the client will not pay an excessive price for doing so. Other law firms may use a different approach, but that/those other approaches impose an unfair burden on the client. Again, make sure that your new attorney reduces the fee by any amounts owed to the prior attorney.

Can Medical Bills Be Negotiated by an Attorney?

Yes, they can be negotiated by the attorney at no extra charge. In other words, liens are a fact of life in these cases. They come about either through a worker's compensation lien or they come about through a medical lien. These liens can be negotiated as part of the third party settlement.

The third party settlement net to the client is reduced by the fee and expenses and by any liens that have to be paid. An experienced personal injury attorney will work avidly on behalf of the client to make sure that he/she can net as much as possible. One way to do that is to reduce the lien. Another negotiating strategy is to say to the lienholder as follows:

"Look, the client won't take the offer if [he/she] is going to net such a reduced amount on account of your lien. It just won't put enough in [his or her] pocket. Therefore, you are going to have to do more on the lien [i.e. reduce it]. If you don't do more on the lien, the case will be tried and if we should lose it, you won't get anything back."

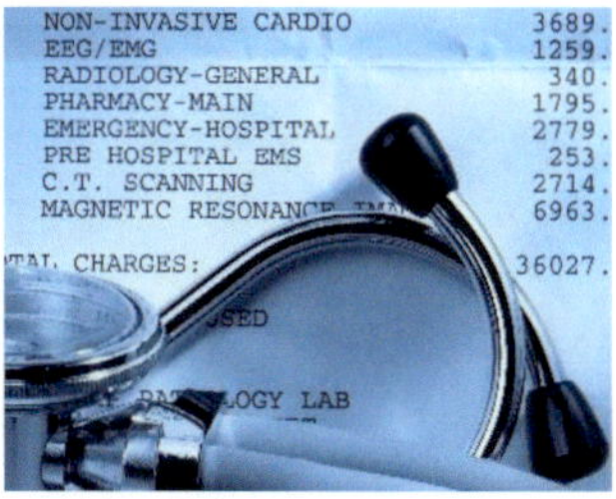

That often proves very useful in getting a reduction and in thereby increasing the client's net recovery.

Why Most Personal Injury Cases Settle Before Going To Trial

Over 90% of personal injury cases do settle before trial. However, it is said, and I must agree, that if you prepare a case to settle, it tries; if you prepare a case to try, it settles. Therefore, thorough preparation is more apt to get you a settlement than not. Relatively speaking, very few civil cases are tried in the Massachusetts Superior Courts.

There are many reasons why a case will settle. Eventually, the insurance company knows it's a war of attrition. They are putting money into the case, whether for defense costs or expert costs or both. Sometimes, for their internal accounting procedures, they want to see a case resolved. However, they are also looking at the quality of the opponent, the quality of the lawyer on the other side and they are asking, "Can this lawyer try the case?" If they know the lawyer, and they know that the lawyer can try the case and can try it very well, then they are more apt to settle. It helps the client to be represented by a very well-respected attorney.

All of this goes into the insurance company's calculation of whether a particular case is dangerous for them: a jury will be troubled in a way that helps the plaintiff, the jury will not like the defendant or the conduct of the defendant, and instead they will find the plaintiff sympathetic. Those are factors that will make the insurance company want to settle.

Why do the numbers provided by the Massachusetts Superior Court show such a high percentage of settled cases? The system, I submit, works toward that goal: there is delay which can tire out either party; there is pressure from the judge; there is the risk-adverse feeling of the parties; there are mounting expenses for experts and other financially draining issues; and there are many stops (opportunities) along the way for an end result, i.e. a settlement.

How Long Will A Personal Injury Case Take To Resolve?

I recommend that clients give six to nine months after their injury has been established for the case to be resolved. But the may be wishful thinking in some cases, particularly ones with major injuries. A significant accident may well take a year to two, occasionally longer. An experienced attorney will work to have the case resolved quickly. But that statement comes with a caveat. A big caveat. A significant case can take a lot longer despite the best of intentions. I will tell you this: any delay will not be because I drag my feet. I work on a limited number of cases at a time, cases that I can hone in on, so the delay will not be attributable to me. But the process can sometimes slow it down.

Going over the court statistics from Fiscal Year 2015, of the 29,000 pending cases in the superior court, only 271 civil cases were tried. That is an easy statistic to follow.

50% of the 29,000 active cases are pending for less than a year. This shows that there is a good "throughput," the number of cases entered versus number of cases that resolve in a given year. Around 20,000 cases will resolve in a given year.

The factors of each case will determine the speed. A lot will depend on how strenuously liability is fought and, in other instances, how long the injury takes to be clarified and properly forecasted. The more the argument is waged around liability, the longer the delay because fault will have to get straightened out in discovery or litigation. If an insurer thinks it has a strong defense on liability, they will not be inclined to pay, and certainly not inclined to make a quick and fair settlement offer in those situations. I tell my clients to let the facts emerge in discovery and, then if they develop properly, it will be time enough to negotiate. It will surely be a better time than it was before liability was established.

29,000 CIVIL CASES AND COUNTING...

On the website of the Massachusetts Courts is a wealth of information. Since my practice is primarily focused in the Superior Courts where the assessed value of cases is $25,000 or more and since I only do civil cases, I looked at those numbers very carefully.

Let's review the last chapter briefly. We see that there are about 29,000 active cases in the Massachusetts Superior Courts. This is statewide. It is interesting because an almost equal number of cases are disposed of as are filed in a given year. That is the "throughput," as we have learned meaning that there are 29,000 active civil cases at the end of the year as at the beginning of the year.

Now something of great interest to lawyers is the number of cases that were tried to a jury. Yes, there were only 271 jury trials in Superior Court for civil cases out of a total caseload of 29,000. You may ask if that is so, why do I speak of trials so often? Well, even though the percentage of cases that are tried is less than 1%, a case will be assessed by how well it will "play" before a jury. I have said repeatedly that cases are always being looked at from the long view - how will the person appear in front of a jury, how will the case sound to a jury, what is the defense, how credible is the defendant or key witnesses. Yes, even with a very small number of cases being tried, we still need to look at those things. A case will be assessed as “if it were to go the distance.”

The district courts, the lower courts, have 79,000 pending civil cases. Interestingly, that figure has dropped markedly and steadily over the last 5 years, down from 123,000 five years ago. That is a drop of almost 50,000. I do not know why that is and I look forward to an explanation.

These are things to consider when asking yourself whether you will have a jury trial, the speed in which you can expect resolution of your case, and whether there is in fact a backlog in the courts. I will argue that there is no real backlog of cases at least in terms of the Superior Court and in terms of civil cases. In the subsequent chapter, we will examine the duration of a case: that is, from filing in the court to conclusion. On the whole, those figures are encouraging.

Below is a synopsis of the relevant statistics from the Massachusetts Courts as of 2015:

In the District and Municipal Courts: filings are down from 123,447 in 2011 to 79,993.

In the Superior Courts civil cases: 28,994 are active, pending cases, close to the statistics in each of the last several years.

Of those active, pending cases in the Superior Courts: 22,230 were entered in 2015.

Of the 19,789 cases that were disposed in 2015: 271 were tried to a jury verdict.

I always find that clients, like doctors' patients, do better when informed. It can create anxiety but on the whole a detailed picture will give you an idea of what to expect. While progress has been made in the courts on reducing the backlog of cases, more can be done. In subsequent chapters, I will discuss what, if anything, your lawyer can do to resolve your case in a timely fashion having in mind that you want and deserve full value for your personal injury case. Quick resolution and obtaining maximum value can be two goals that are in conflict with one another.

What To Expect: The Age Of Civil Cases In Massachusetts

In this chapter, I will discuss how long the 29,000 civil cases have been active in the Superior Courts across Massachusetts, something not covered in detail in the statistics-laden last two chapters. I can provide an optimistic view (at least compared to prior eras) of how long you should expect your case to take.

How long have those cases been pending? I find this particularly interesting because when I started practicing law in the 1980s there really was a court backlog. You could wait five years to get a typical personal injury case tried. Now, there are some cases that are old. For the most part, however, I don't see the serious backlog any longer. I certainly don't hear of the aptly named "strangulation list" that used to exist in Suffolk County, Boston's county.

For a long time, the Justices have been very concerned that there not be a backlog. Statistics are meticulously kept. Attention is paid to the "through-put", that previously discussed arithmetic comparison of cases entered versus cases disposed. The "through-put" rate has been very good, indicating that virtually as many cases are disposed as compared to the number that are filed in a given year. Recall the statistics in the last chapter.

According to Fiscal Year 2015 statistics, about 13,500 of the pending civil cases in Massachusetts Superior Courts are a year or newer. The rest are anywhere from 1-5 years but the bulk of the remainder are really 1-3 years old. About 12,500 of those are pending cases that have been in the court system for that 1-3 year period. Therefore, 26,000 of the 29,000 active civil cases in the Massachusetts Superior Courts have been pending for no more than three years. Those are pretty good numbers, I would suggest.

If you have a serious personal injury case, it should be brought in the Superior Court. As you can see, you have good reason to believe that it will be resolved within three years and possibly even resolved within one year. I suggest to you that this is a dramatic difference from what we saw thirty years ago. That is a fortunate thing. As the old saying goes, justice delayed is justice denied.

By all means, the Courts can do even better and there are many committees that are focusing on the speed in which cases are resolved. But quick resolution can be particularly challenging in an era of reduced court resources. The courts are often an easy target in which a cost-conscious legislature may want to find areas to cut. Those disputes among the branches of government are not especially of concern to me and probably of little interest to you. It is important to note, however, that the size of the Judiciary and its staff are not growing. In fact, some Superior Court sessions have been forced in recent years to use law school graduates for volunteer clerkships. This would be unheard of in the Federal Courts. These inexperienced and unpaid individuals will help the Judges draft Memoranda and do other research. There are no secretaries available anymore.

With that in mind, the relative speed - I say relative, please note - of resolution is impressive.

Of course, if you have a serious personal injury case, it is your case and statistics may not be comforting. To that I can say two things: ask your lawyer for an update and a realistic timetable so that you can plan accordingly, and be consoled by the facts that your case is being litigated in the 2010s and not the 1980s. Maybe the 2020s will be even better.

Housekeeping Matters At The Conclusion Of Your Case

The final chapter will discuss the issues confronting a client when his/her civil personal injury case resolves. At the outset of the representation, there should have been a discussion of fees and expenses so that there will be no surprises. This understanding should also have been memorialized in the Contingent Fee Agreement. Does the attorney expect the case expenses to be paid by the client as they are incurred or does the attorney expect reimbursement upon the conclusion of the case? If the attorney does not expect reimbursement until the end of the case, there is still the question of whether reimbursement is dependent on the outcome of the case.

As I have stated in several previous chapters, my firm's policy is to ask the client for reimbursement only upon conclusion of the matter. Again, I only expect reimbursement if the case is resolved successfully. Thus, my firm will cover these expenses in the unlikely event that the case yields no reward. Assuming a successful settlement or verdict, my office will go through our books and we will have our bookkeeper present the client with a list of expenses. We will, if asked, discuss these expenses with the client and explain why they were necessary in achieving the desired outcome. Additionally, we can provide actual invoices.

The expenses come out of the client's share, as does the fee. As I explained in a previous chapter, this is a contingent fee, rather than an hourly one, and that is beneficial to clients. The contingent fee system has been declared "the poor man's key to the courthouse." Whether the client is poor or not, most people are happy not to worry about ongoing legal bills. And I am happy not to bill clients in the traditional way.

With respect to those dreaded and dreadful liens, our office spends a good deal of time on that aspect of closing a file. In recent years, we have been very successful in eliminating from the lien charges that arguably don't relate to the injury for which a recovery was awarded. As an example, if a client suffered multiple injuries but the third-party insurer acknowledged only one of those injuries in the negotiation, then only the treatment for the compensated part of the injury is properly included in the final lien. I have even asked the liability insurer to provide corroboration to the medical lien holder so the lien holder will see what I am saying is true. The result has been favorable on eliminating many charges on the lien.

There are other liens and obstacles that can occur: worker's compensation liens, set offs pursuant to a complicated doctrine in Massachusetts known as the Hunter offset, and Medicare set-asides, to name just three. Lastly, it is important for clients to understand that some settlements may be conducive to a structured settlement. Some clients may prefer a long payout as discussed previously.

In more than a few cases, issues have come up long after the case has resolved. Our firm prides itself on continuing to work with the former client. All it requires is a phone call. The client has every right to expect a supportive lawyer on the other end of the call - one who has not forgotten the client. Hopefully, if you are in that situation, you will not hesitate to call Feinberg and Alban. We will do our best to help as we would have done throughout the life of the case.

Disclaimer

This publication is intended to be informational only. No legal advice is being given, and no attorney-client relationship is intended to be created by reading this material. If you are facing legal issues, whether criminal or civil, seek professional legal counsel to get your questions answered.

Feinberg & Alban, P.C.
225 Franklin Street, 26th Floor
Boston, MA 02110

1051 Beacon Street
Brookline, MA, 02446

(617) 232-5950
www.feinbergalban.com

Made in the USA
Monee, IL
05 November 2026

67386567R00057